IMAGES
of America

SANTA MARIA VALLEY

A 1946 aerial view of Santa Maria shows large agricultural fields in and around the city. At the bottom is the unincorporated town of Orcutt, and in the background are the rolling hills north of Nipomo and the tops of the La Panza Range. At the middle left is the city's 39-plus-acre fairgrounds on West Stowell Road. The site was purchased in 1941 for $35,000.

ON THE COVER: The Gray family riding team appears during the 11th Annual Elks Rodeo Parade in 1954 on Broadway. The event was announced as "the largest rodeo parade in Santa Maria rodeo history." From left to right are Joe Gray, Dorothy Gray, Joni Gray, and Norma Gray. (Courtesy of Santa Maria Elks Lodge 1538 History Committee.)

IMAGES
of America

SANTA MARIA VALLEY

Carina Monica Montoya and the
Santa Maria Valley Historical Society

ARCADIA
PUBLISHING

Published by Arcadia Publishing
Charleston, South Carolina

Library of Congress Control Number: 2011928027

For all general information, please contact Arcadia Publishing:
Telephone 843-853-2070
Fax 843-853-0044
E-mail sales@arcadiapublishing.com
For customer service and orders:
Toll-Free 1-888-313-2665

Visit us on the Internet at www.arcadiapublishing.com

*In memory of Clarence S. Minetti (1918–2011), one of
Santa Maria Valley's most beloved residents, restaurateur,
community leader, cowboy, and friend*

CONTENTS

Foreword   6

Acknowledgments   7

Introduction   8

1.   Historical Eras: Mexican (1821–1848) and American
     (1848–Present)   11

2.   The Green Valley: World-Famous Flower Seeds,
     Strawberries, and Produce   39

3.   Sports: Major Leagues and the Olympics   55

4.   Community Spirit: Patriotism, Clubs, and Organizations   63

5.   Planes and Trains: Historic Flights and One of the
     Busiest Short Lines in the Country   77

6.   Reflections: Looking Back Over the Years   87

7.   A Glimpse Around Town: Santa Maria Today   109

FOREWORD

I was born and raised in Santa Maria. My parents, Laurence and Helen, married in 1926 and moved from San Francisco to Santa Maria in 1934. My dad was the assistant manager for Bank of America's Santa Maria branch. It was June 1953 when I graduated from Santa Maria High School. For me, it was held in the Ethel Pope Auditorium, surrounded by friends, classmates, and family. Many of them were excited to graduate and leave Santa Maria for new jobs and new adventures. I, too, would be leaving, but knew that I would be returning.

Looking through this wonderful book brings back memories. The majority of photographs have never before been published. Thanks go to the Santa Maria Historical Society Museum, for sharing much of its priceless trove of photographs, and to Carina Montoya, for her fine eye in crafting this book. As the saying goes, a picture is worth a thousand words. Leafing through these pages, we are reminded that Santa Maria was built by many people, often with no recognition or great material rewards. We are fortunate to be standing on their shoulders.

During World War II, I watched with my parents as Stearmans and other planes landed at Hancock Field, where Allan Hancock College now stands. As a young man, I fondly recall cruising Broadway in my red Triumph TR3, purchased from a Santa Maria dealership. The town was much smaller back then; there were fields south of Stowell Road and no homes to the north, near the river.

Santa Maria is my home. A lot has changed over the decades, but I still consider Santa Maria the best place anyone could live. The town of 10,000 that I remember as a teenager is now a community with 100,000 residents. As a boy, I never thought politics was in my future. To be the mayor of a town where I have lived my whole life is very exciting. One of the first people to congratulate me was someone I had gone through school with from the first grade.

In recent years, some of the iconic figures in Santa Maria's history have gone on to their great reward. Their passing gives us occasion to reflect on their accomplishments and contributions. It is so important and interesting to remember how our community has evolved. This book is a valuable insight into our past.

—Larry Lavagnino, mayor of Santa Maria

ACKNOWLEDGMENTS

My heartfelt gratitude goes to Richard Chenoweth, longtime resident of Santa Maria and director of the Santa Maria Historical Society Museum. His generous support in supplying resources and information was invaluable in the compilation of materials necessary for the writing of this book. I want to especially thank my acquistions and production editors at Arcadia Publishing: Jerry Roberts, for his support in my ideas and proposal; Debbie Seracini, for her professional guidance; and Tim Sumerel, for his thorough proofing and edits.

My deepest appreciation goes to the Santa Maria Valley Historical Society and its board of directors: Jim Zemaitis, Jim Enos, Hal Madson, Jim O'Neill, Dave Carey, Shirley Contreras, Ginger Reeves, Joanne McBride, Dave Cross, Gloria Mornard, Myrna Winter, John Everett, and Dee Martini; and to Tommy Gee and the Santa Maria Elks Lodge 1538 History Committee, for their generous contribution of photographs.

I am especially grateful to the Honorable Laurence J. Lavagnino, mayor of the city of Santa Maria, for his contribution in writing the foreword to this book.

I am indebted to Steven De La Vega, for his invaluable assistance in the scanning of hundreds of photographs; Janice Featherston, for her generous photography services; and Rancho de Guadalupe Historical Society and its board of directors: Richard Pelton, John Perry, Mary Harris, Dolores Pelton, Elva Alvarez, Mabel Arellanes, Shirley Boydstun, George McMillin, and Stephanie Krouse.

Special thanks go to Dorothy Benford; Jamie Bennett; the City of Santa Maria; Santino De La Vega; Dudley-Hoffman; Bob McCutcheon; Sandhya Ramadas, Esq.; Eric Spies; Madison Stanford; Mark Steller; Barbara Tell; and Louis Escobar, owner of Reflections Photography.

A special acknowledgment goes to my mother, Rose Q. Montoya, who was the biggest supporter in all my undertakings, including this book, but passed away on December 31, 2010, before the book's publication.

Unless otherwise noted, all images appear courtesy of the Santa Maria Valley Historical Society Museum. In chapter seven, unless otherwise noted, all images are courtesy of Janice Featherston.

INTRODUCTION

Long before Spanish explorer Gaspar de Portolá trekked through Santa Maria in 1769 on an expedition that spanned California's coast from San Diego to Monterey, the native inhabitants of the Central Coast were Chumash Indians. Located in the heart of California's Central Coast, the Santa Maria Valley blankets an area in Santa Barbara County that is bounded on the north by the hills north of Nipomo, on the northeast by the tops of the La Panza Range in the Los Padres National Forest, southeastward by the crest of the Sierra Madre intersecting the San Rafael Wilderness, and to the south with the high points in the Purisima Hills north of Los Olivos. The Chumash established settlements in the hills around the valley and along the coast, where wild game and seafood were plentiful. The valley's rich resources of water and oil remained hidden under its wild, dry, and desolate floor until settlement began with the establishment of Mission San Luis Obispo to the north in 1772 and La Purisima Conception in 1787, located southwest of Santa Maria, as well as other events that would later attract more migrations to the valley.

For several years, the valley was merely a rugged, windblown, and dry passageway used to get to other parts of the state. In the 1700s, on their journey to find Monterey Bay, Spanish expeditions traveled a dirt trail that passed through the valley. It was later named the California Mission Trail because it linked California's 21 missions, presidios, and pueblos from San Diego to Sonoma. The Spanish called the dry valley El Llano Large de Laguna, meaning "the long valley of the lagoon." In the mid-1800s, it was a route prospectors stampeded through on their way to wherever gold was reported to be found.

With Mexico's independence in 1821, missions became secularized, and mission-owned lands were broken up into large ranchos and granted out for individual landownership. The grants were typically given to former soldiers, or their descendants, for loyal service during the war. This significant event attracted people to the Central Coast in hopes of obtaining free land. From this era came the Mexican vaqueros, who worked on the ranchos. They were the first cowboys who were highly skilled in cattle herding. Early American cowboys learned how to rope and handle cattle from these skilled horsemen, and many of those techniques are still used today. The Santa Maria barbecue also has its roots in the early rancho days, when friends and neighbors would gather for a Spanish-style outdoor meal, consisting of meat cooked in an earthen pit over native red oak.

In 1837, William Benjamin Foxen and his wife, Eduarda (née Osuna), were granted the 8,874-acre Rancho Tinaquaic and became the first non-Indian settlers in the valley. In 1875, Foxen's daughter Ramona and her husband, Frederick Wickenden, built the Chapel of San Ramon and began its cemetery on a knoll that overlooks the upper Santa Maria Valley, where both Benjamin and Eduarda are now buried. The chapel was one of the first Catholic churches in the Santa Maria Valley, and its architecture is characteristic of Early American style, with the use of wood in creating strong, simple forms replacing the adobe formerly widely used in California. A century later, the Chapel of San Ramon was renamed San Ramon Chapel and dedicated as Santa Barbara County Landmark No. 1 and California State Landmark No. 877.

In 1856, Juan Pacifico Ontiveros and his wife, Martina, purchased the Rancho Tepusquet. Juan was a skilled ranchero, driving more than 1,000 head of cattle from Southern California to his Tepusquet property and selling them to drovers throughout the year. He named a nearby waterway Santa Maria Creek, which is now known as the Santa Maria River. They also named their home Santa Maria, which was likely in honor of the Virgin Mary, mother of Jesus. Unbeknownst to them at the time, it would later become the name of a town.

Early settlers began to tap local water sources and were farming the area by the time California became a state in 1850. Beans and grains were the main crops in the early years, because they were more drought-tolerant than fruits and vegetables. Farming in the valley began to attract more farmers and settlers, turning the small dirt mission trail into a main vein of north-south stagecoach travel. The first town in the valley was La Graciosa, meaning "the graceful," near present-day Orcutt. Its post office, store, and stagecoach station shared one building. The town also had a school. Oil would later be discovered in and around the Orcutt area, resulting in the valley's oil industry flourishing for the next 80 years. However, the town of La Graciosa did not. The land upon which the town was built was sold, and the new owner's plans to redevelop the area forced La Graciosa residents and business owners to leave.

Between the years 1869 and 1874, Rudolph Cook, John Thornburg, Isaac Fesler, and Isaac Miller each homesteaded several acres of land in the valley. They all agreed to donate a square mile of their land where their properties met to form a four-square-mile town center, resulting in a township that was surveyed in 1874 and officially recorded with the county as the town of Grangeville in 1875. The intersection where the four corners met became Main Street and Broadway. However, the town's name soon changed to Central City, because of its midway location between the community of Guadalupe and Sisquoc, but the new name caused problems with the post office, because mail intended for the valley was sent to Central City, Colorado, which had been established first. Central City, California, was a thriving community that hosted a blacksmith, wagon and machine shop, steam-fed mill, lumberyard, and the Hart House hotel, all built by English immigrant Reuben Hart. The Reuben Hart residence was built in 1877 on Church Street and is one of the oldest houses in Santa Maria.

By 1882, the narrow gauge Pacific Coast Railway from San Luis Obispo to Central City came into existence, and Central City was renamed Santa Maria. In 1901, the Southern Pacific Railroad traveled the lower part of the valley to Los Angeles, and by 1912, the Santa Maria Valley Railroad linked the oilfields at Roadamite to Guadalupe.

Adding to the already growing ethnic groups in the town, which included Spanish, Mexican, English, Scottish, Irish, and Japanese, many Swiss-Italians and Portuguese settled in the valley. They established large dairy farms and other businesses in both Guadalupe and Santa Maria that serviced the valley for decades. Advanced methods of irrigation transformed the valley into one of California's most fertile garden plots, producing world-famous flower seeds, strawberries, lettuce, broccoli, cauliflower, and many other fruits and vegetables. The family names of some of these early immigrant settlers are still familiar and revered in the community. They include, but are not limited to, Aratani, Minami, Olivera, Righetti, Rusconi, Teixeria, Tognazzini, and Waller, to name only a few.

Santa Maria's many landmarks include Buena Vista Park, the oldest park in Santa Maria, and the flagpole at the George S. Hobbs's Civic Center, located at South Broadway and East Cook Street. Dedicated in August 1918 in honor of Santa Maria Valley men and women who were serving in World War I, its original location was at the intersection of Main Street and Broadway. In 1942, it was moved to its present site, considered a more suitable place, away from the intersection, where it interfered with traffic, particularly large military vehicles. Other landmarks include the site of the city's first waterworks in 1880; the Reuben Hart residence; the 1882 railroad depot site; the Santa Maria Inn, founded in 1917; and city hall, dedicated in 1934.

By the 20th century, Santa Maria was widely known for its fertile soil and moderate climate. In the early years, farming was necessary to feed one's family. However, the agricultural industry in the valley grew to supply parts of the country as far away as the Atlantic coast and developed a means to transport produce to arrive fresh at its destination. Japanese immigrant Setsuo Aratani pioneered the vegetable industry in both growing and ice-transport methods. Capt. G. Allan Hancock would later come to the valley and add an ice plant. Hancock also founded Rosemary Farm, one of California's oldest egg distributors, and purchased the Santa Maria Valley Railroad, which became the country's busiest short-line railway. In addition to Hancock's many financial contributions and improvements to the Santa Maria Valley, his interest in aeronautics played a vital role in attracting more people and businesses to the area. He financed the historic *Southern Cross* flight in 1928 and founded the Hancock College of Aeronautics that provided ground and flight training to thousands of pilots during World War II. Santa Maria Community College later occupied the aeronautic college and was renamed Hancock College in honor of Capt. G. Allan Hancock.

Sports have been a big part of the Santa Maria community since the late 1800s—especially baseball. Among the many local valley baseball teams, the Santa Maria Indians semiprofessional team included players who later signed on with major league teams throughout the country. Setsuo Aratani was a baseball enthusiast, and in 1928, he sponsored a team to compete in Japan. John Madden, who coached football at Hancock Junior College, went on to become the country's most recognized voice in professional football broadcasting. John Paulsen and Eugene Lenz went on to compete in the Summer Olympics in 1932 and 1960, respectively; and many other Santa Maria homegrown star athletes went on to play on bigger fields.

Santa Maria was incorporated as a municipal corporation of the sixth class in 1905, and by the time the city celebrated its centennial on September 12, 2005, the small dirt mission trail had long been transformed into a major California interstate highway. The mission trail is regarded as one of California's most significant landmarks, stretching from Mission San Diego de Alcala to Mission San Francisco de Asis. Distinctive bells that hang on supports resembling a shepherd's crook, or a Franciscan walking stick, memorializing California's Spanish history, dot the long stretch of highway, with one located in Santa Maria and one in Guadalupe.

Today, Santa Maria still produces some of the country's choicest fruits and vegetables, and because of its rare transverse geography, is recognized as one of the world's most dynamic wine-growing regions. In addition to agriculture, the valley has become home to many businesses in the fields of aerospace, communications, high-tech research and development, energy production, and manufacturing. The Guadalupe-Nipomo Dunes, covering 22,000 acres and 18 miles, are the largest coastal dunes in California. Designation as a national wildlife refuge ensures the long-term protection of the dunes' many natural resources, wildlife, and endangered bird species. Because of its towering dunes and overall picturesque landscape that includes green fields, rolling hills, and the Pacific Ocean, it is also a popular location for Hollywood filmmakers. Among many other motion pictures throughout the years, Cecil B. DeMille's 1923 movie *The Ten Commandments* was filmed on the dunes, and a large segment of the dunes was featured in the 2006 film *Pirates of the Caribbean: Dead Man's Chest*.

Santa Maria won an All-America City Award from the National Civic League in 1998, honoring the city as "a better place to live and work." The Santa Maria Valley is truly one of California's prized gems. Its long, colorful history is found in stories and legends about the Old West covering topics such as native Indians, stagecoach holdups, whiskey saloons, droughts, fires, floods, and Solomon Pico, on whom the legend of Zorro is based.

Within the pages of this small book is a glimpse of a once-small farming community that grew into becoming the largest populated and most enterprising city in Santa Barbara County. The Santa Maria Valley Historical Society and Museum is dedicated to the gathering and preservation of the valley's important and rich history. While the people of the valley continue to look forward to future growth, they embrace its past with pride, which was my inspiration in the writing of this book.

One

HISTORICAL ERAS
MEXICAN (1821–1848) AND
AMERICAN (1848–PRESENT)

When Mexico won independence from Spain in 1821, missions became secularized, and mission-owned lands were broken up into large ranchos and granted to Mexican citizens, typically to former soldiers or their descendants, for loyal service during the Spanish-Mexican War. Teodoro Arellanes and Don Diego Olivera were granted the 43,682-acre Rancho Guadalupe around the mid-1800s. Another land grant in the valley was Rancho Tinaquaic, granted to Benjamin Foxen and his wife, Eduarda del Carmen Osuna, the first non-Indian settlers in the valley. Other land grants included 4,459 acres of El Rincon and 26,648 acres of Punta de la Laguna. Early adobe houses were typically small and flat-roofed, but by the mid-1800s, two-story structures called Monterey adobes were replacing the traditional rectangular or box shape. Later, adobe houses had clay tiles or wood-shake roofs and covered porches with *corredores*, either in the front of the house or encircling the entire house. The newer adobes with gabled, wood-structured roofs evidenced Early American influence in their construction.

When California became a state in 1850, the arrival of settlers marked the birth of the town and the beginning of the end of the rancho era. Farming proved to be difficult, and although rain and local water sources provided some irrigation, it was not sufficient for growing fruits and vegetables. Beans and grains were the main crops in the early years, because they were more drought-resistant. Later, steam-powered farm equipment, milling facilities, and the railroad opened the gates to increased commerce. The town's first name was Grangeville, or Grangerville, named after a local Grangeville store; it was later renamed Central City. Central City's main downtown area was located on Broadway and Main Street, where saloons, mercantiles, barbershops, and hotels sprouted up. The contributions of the early immigrants laid the cornerstone in the building and development of the valley, bringing skills and talents in blacksmithing, construction, farming, dairying, and planting. They paved the road that would lead to Santa Maria.

An unidentified man stands in front of the Ontiveros adobe, built in 1858, on the Tepusquet Rancho in the 1920s. Although Ontiveros served in the Spanish army, he and his wife, Martina, purchased the rancho in 1856. A skilled cattleman, Ontiveros and his sons drove 1,200 cattle from Southern California to the rancho, selling them to drovers throughout the year. Juan died in 1877 and Martina in 1897.

Built on a knoll in 1875, the Chapel of San Ramon in Sisquoc was one of the first Catholic churches in the Santa Maria Valley. Its architecture is classic Early American. A century later, the chapel was renamed San Ramon Chapel and dedicated as Santa Barbara County Landmark No. 1 and California State Landmark No. 877.

In 1879, the Morris family arrived in Central City in a covered wagon. It was the same year that entrepreneur Reuben Hart, an English immigrant, built the town's waterworks. Central City was a fast-growing town with many businesses built along Broadway and Main Street. Within 13 years of Hart's arrival, he had constructed the town's first brick building. It housed a blacksmith, wagon and machine shop, a steam-fed mill with an outdoor lumberyard, and a hotel.

A crew of threshers is shown in the late 1800s. Threshing separates grain from chaff, and early methods required a minimum of five workers to cut twined bundles, feed the bundles into the machine, operate the stacker, maintain the machine, and bag the grain. It was common on threshing day to have a crew of 10 to 12 men, because once the machine was in operation, it had to be continually fed.

A young family helps on threshing day in the late 1800s, saving the cost of hiring a full crew. In the early days, American families were typically large and helped cut farming costs. The early method of mechanized threshing used horsepower by hitching animals to a treadmill, or master wheel, on a rotating horse walker. The horsepower generated was transmitted to rotational shaft power that was connected to the threshing machine.

By the mid- to late 1800s, the use of self-propelled, portable steam engines, also called road locomotives (to distinguish them from steam-powered railroad locomotives), were able to plow fields and move heavy loads. They were large and heavy in comparison to the man in the buggy (right), and although they were slow and did not maneuver well, portable steam engines revolutionized farming and transport by replacing draft horses.

At a Pacific Coast Railway warehouse on North Depot Street in Santa Maria, beans and grains are stacked alongside the tracks of the narrow gauge rail line. It was common for warehouses to be overfilled, forcing the surplus sacks to be stored outside during summer months, as seen in the 1907 photograph above and the picture of the Guadalupe warehouse in the late 1800s below. (Both, courtesy of Rancho de Guadalupe Historical Society & Museum.)

A team of 10 is used to harvest sugar beets in Betteravia for the Union Sugar Company, founded on the former Rancho Punta de Laguna in the early 1900s. Sugar beets were among the hardiest crops and were widely planted in Betteravia, Guadalupe, Santa Maria, and Orcutt. Early methods of harvesting were by hand, and transport to receiving stations was by horse-drawn apparatuses.

These two mule-drawn teams, with filled wagons of harvested sugar beets, await arrival of the train at this receiving station in Betteravia in the early 1900s. The beets will be transported to the Union Sugar Company, where they will be converted to granulated sugar. The drivers of the teams are standing atop their wagons because hauling wagons had no seats.

Pinal Oil Company was founded in Santa Maria in 1901. In 1911, the company merged with Dome Oil Company to form the Pinal Dome Oil Company, which was bought by Union Oil in July 1917. Having 22 wells in production by 1903, Union Oil was the major oil company in the valley. With thousands of smaller wells in production, the valley's oil industry flourished for 80 years.

Pinal Oil workers in 1907 cart oil drums by wagon to Orcutt Depot for transport on the Pacific Coast Company Railroad, which served the West Coast from the mid-1800s until it was sold in the mid-1900s.

1912 · ROY HIESIE – UNION OIL CO. ENGINEER (WITH WATER BAG) HE BUILT THE HARTNELL PLANT

In 1912, Roy Hiesie (holding water bag) was an engineer for Union Oil Company and built Hartnell Well No. 1, commonly known as Old Maud. Old Maud was discovered by accident, but it proved to be the largest oil-bearing reservoir in the area, producing one million barrels of oil in its first 100 days of operation. As seen in the background, oil structures in the early years were built of wood.

By the early 1900s, Santa Maria saw significant developments in not only in farming but also arts and culture. The Minerva Club, a local women's group, was founded in the spirit of educating women, who were otherwise relegated to housekeeping. These efforts led to the city's first library. Members of the Masonic lodge are pictured in 1908 performing the ceremonial laying of the cornerstone for the new Carnegie library.

An unidentified man stands in front of the 1911 brick building in downtown Orcutt in the 1910s. The Orcutt branch of the Bank of Santa Maria is seen next door. The Bank of Santa Maria was founded in 1890 and became the First National Bank of Santa Maria five years later.

Downtown Guadalupe is pictured in 1914. The Union Livery Stable and Garage can be seen on the left. Guadalupe is one of the valley's oldest communities. From its beginning, the town was a small farming community, with several dairies, many established by Swiss-Italian immigrants. Across the street is the two-story Commercial Hotel (later the Basque House restaurant), at the corner of Tenth and Guadalupe Streets. (Courtesy of Rancho de Guadalupe Historical Society & Museum.)

A large structure for its time, the Guadalupe School was built in 1897 and operated for 33 years. It was the second elementary school in the town. Standing out front and on the second-floor balcony in the early 1900s are the students and teachers. (Courtesy of Rancho de Guadalupe Historical Society & Museum.)

Children appear outside a public schoolhouse in Betteravia in the early 1900s. Teachers can be seen standing in the back, at right. The arrival of the Union Sugar Company in the late 1800s and subsequent establishment of the Betteravia community included a school. Children of the employees of Union Sugar and surrounding farms attended classes there.

Pauline Stockhausen (left) and Irene Alliani sit in an open, horse-drawn buggy in downtown Guadalupe in the early 1900s. The Old Brewery, one of the town's bars, can be seen in the background. (Courtesy of Rancho de Guadalupe Historical Society & Museum.)

Although the long hair and dress style would suggest that these two young children in this early-1900s photograph are girls, they are two young boys in Guadalupe. It was common in those days for young boys to wear tunics and long stockings. Across the street behind them are the J.B. Acquistapage General Merchandise store and the Secondo Veglia Saloon, one of Guadalupe's many early establishments that sold alcohol prior to Prohibition in 1920. (Courtesy of Rancho de Guadalupe Historical Society & Museum.)

Founded by Reuben Hart and built by the Doane Building Company in 1888, the Hart House (above) was the town's first grand hotel, located on the southeast corner of East Main Street and Broadway. It opened with a gala reception and became Santa Maria's most popular establishment, with a barbershop, reading room, retail shops, and a bar. The Hart House's many first-class services included a covered carriage, providing local transportation services (below). It served as a shuttle to pick up and drop off visitors to and from nearby train depots. The hotel was later sold and became the Bradley Hotel, which was destroyed by fire on April 25, 1970.

The Campodonico Mercantile was one of the early businesses established in Guadalupe in the late 1800s. It was a general store that sold groceries, household items, and personal accessories. Pictured from left to right are Waldo Grisingher, Albert Juarez, Joe Feliciano, Hazen Baumgartner, and Stephen V. Campodonico (behind the counter). (Courtesy of Rancho de Guadalupe Historical Society & Museum.)

M. Fleisher & Co. was a Santa Maria business that sold grain and beans, as seen on the early-1900s sign. Grain and beans were important crops in the early years, when irrigation methods were not yet fully developed. They were more drought-tolerant and were widely farmed. Next door is Sutherland & Co., a store that sold fruits, vegetables, groceries, and grain.

The infamous Whiskey Row was once located in the four-corners section of downtown, which spanned across the first block of East Main Street. John Thornburg, one of four founding fathers who established the four corners, was of Quaker persuasion and would not allow alcohol to be sold near his southwest corner of the intersection. However, Isaac Miller, one of the other founding fathers, favored its consumption and allowed it to be sold on his northeast corner. Whiskey Row's origins date back to Central City in the mid-1880s, and it was off-limits to women. Prohibition closed the bars in the 1920s, but they returned when Prohibition ended in 1933. Some of the popular bars included the Oil Exchange, M and M, Amaral's Café, Palamino Club, Ace Hi Café, and Victory Café, to name a few. Whiskey Row was ultimately declared a redevelopment area by the city council in 1959, and its buildings were slated to be demolished. It later became Central Plaza, a downtown park, which was eventually renamed Union Plaza and dedicated in April 1967.

The Rex Café in the 1930s was located on the corner of Broadway and Main Street and was one of many popular bars. It was known as being not only a bar but also a card room, diner, smoke shop, and men's club (above). A dark mahogany bar with brass footrests and spittoons was a common décor of the time (below).

When William Haslam purchased the interests of Emmett Bryant and James F. Goodwin's general merchandise store in 1889, it became the W.A. Haslam and Company store (above), one of Santa Maria's oldest businesses. The City of Paris shop (below), located on South Broadway and owned by Florence Valenzuela in 1914, specialized in fine hats, dresses, and women's accessories. Other early businesses included A.E. Lutnesdky's watchmaker store; Becker News Depot; and Coblentz & Schwabacher, a company that sold a variety of goods, ranging from onions to finery, on Main Street. Also on West Main Street were Fairbanks, Morse & Co.; G.D. Davis Harness Shop; Louis Hau Hardware; Saladin Music; T.A. Jones & Son furniture and carpet store on South Broadway; and Union Meat Market, owned by Langlois and Walker in the 100 block of South Broadway.

A barber stands in front of mirrored stations made from dark mahogany wood, as seen in this early-1900s shop located on West Main Street. Barbershops were among the first businesses established in the valley, and the spiraling, red-and-white barber pole dates to medieval times, when barbers often served as surgeons. However, by the 18th century, barbering and the medical profession were separate institutions.

Security First National Bank was the second bank opened in the town of Guadalupe, superseding the Bank of Guadalupe that was located across the street in the late 1890s. Seen here is the interior of the small, one-teller-window bank. Standing from left to right in this early-1920s image are Erle Fulghum, Dario Ferini (manager), and Fred Gracia. (Courtesy of Rancho de Guadalupe Historical Society & Museum.)

Before Santa Maria City Hall was established, the first city office was located in the 100 block of South Broadway. In this 1913 photograph, the city's first employees are, from left to right, ? Laughlin, ? Cole, Harry Neel, and Rell Laughlin. The one-room office had two desks and a counter. The office serviced the city in administrative matters in the recording of land deeds, buildings, marriages, births, and deaths.

The Golden State Milk Products Company, known as "the Creamery," was the first creamery established in Guadalupe. Many Swiss-Italian and Portuguese immigrants established large agricultural and dairy farms in both Guadalupe and Santa Maria; these served the valley and other areas for decades. In earlier years, there were more than 60 dairies, including the Sunset Laguna, De Bernardi, Sutti, Ruffoni, Guggia, Tognazzini, Albertoni, Caroni, Tiboni, Freddi, and Dybdah, to name a few. (Courtesy of Rancho de Guadalupe Historical Society & Museum.)

Pictured is Albert Dudley, sitting atop a white hearse drawn by two horses in front of the Dudley-Hoffman Mortuary in 1914. The white hearse was used only for children. A similar black hearse was used for adult funerals. The first burial site in Santa Maria was established in 1872. Later, the Santa Maria Cemetery was established in 1917 as a result of the collective efforts of the local Odd Fellows and Masonic lodges. (Courtesy of Dudley-Hoffman.)

The Dudley-Hoffman Mortuary was established in 1876 as a family-owned enterprise. Today, it is one of the city's oldest businesses still in operation. After a couple of relocations throughout the years, it is currently located on East Stowell Road. (Courtesy of Dudley-Hoffman.)

Women cross the intersection of Main Street and Broadway, where Santa Maria's first bank towers behind them. In 1890, Polish immigrant Paul O. Tietzen and Fred Jack founded the Bank of Santa Maria. Five years later, it became the First National Bank of Santa Maria. A few years later, A.P. Giannini wanted to open a Bank of Italy in town, but when the chain was rejected, he opened the Union National Bank in 1926. He later closed and transferred the business into his new Bank of America, formerly known as Bank of Italy. Other local banks throughout the years included Los Padres, which became part of Wells Fargo in the 1960s; Bank of Santa Maria, which merged with Los Angeles Trust and Savings, which became Security First National, and then Security Pacific National Bank; United California Bank, established in the 1960s from a merger between First Western Bank and Trust Company and California Bank, founded by Allan Hancock in 1923; Crocker Anglo National Bank, later Crocker National Bank in 1962; Mid-State Bank in 1970; and a new Bank of Santa Maria in the 1970s.

Gracing the entrance to the Santa Maria Country Club are two 10-foot-high plaster sphinxes, weighing five tons each and taken from the set of the 1923 silent epic *The Ten Commandments*, filmed at the Guadalupe Dunes. When the desert scenes were completed, the $1.4 million Egyptian civilization set was left on the dunes and was buried by sand in much less time than it took to build it.

Downtown Santa Maria is pictured in the mid-1920s. A wooden cross in the middle of the street is marked "Old Tires" and has old tires hooped at its base. From front right to back are the First National Bank, post office, and Santa Maria Chamber of Commerce. Across the street, from front to back, are the Telephone Company and Electric Company. In the far back, the town's first flagpole can be seen in the center of the intersection of Main Street and Broadway.

Founded in 1924, the *Santa Maria Daily Times* operated until 1930. During its six years of operation, the early newspaper kept residents informed of events, including the reporting of "16,500 acres of valley property to be leased by oil companies in 1929." Its staff of writers, editors, printers, and delivery boys is seen in front of the Daily Times Building in this late-1920s photograph.

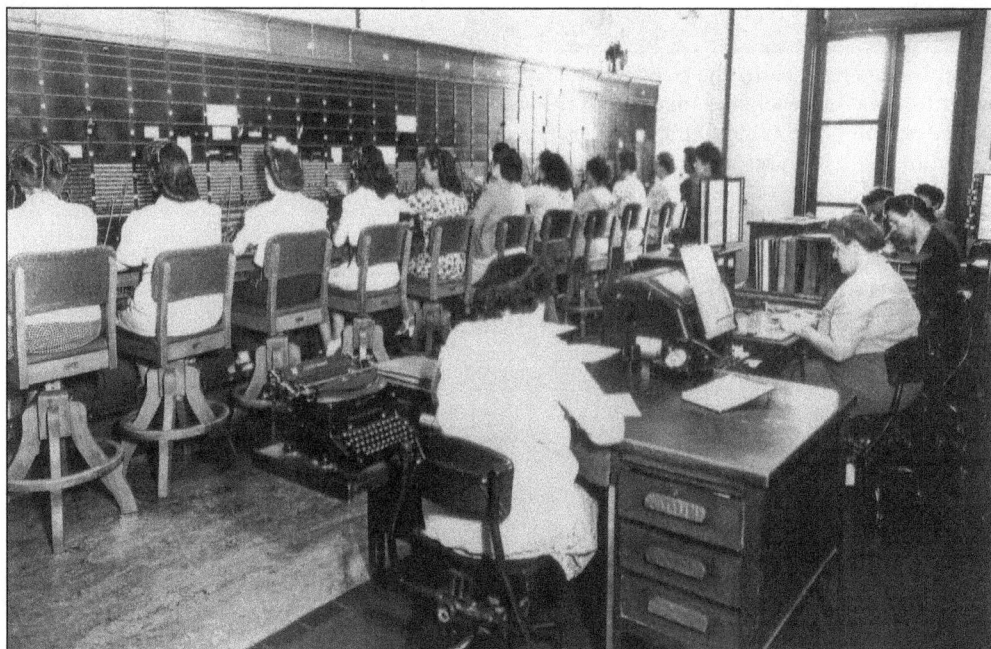

Santa Maria was introduced to its first telephone service by the Sunset Company in 1891. It was a small operation that closed in the evenings. The early telephone office was located in the basement of the first Masonic building in Santa Maria around 1906. Santa Barbara Telephone Company acquired the company in 1917, and General Telephone took over in 1939. By 1950, the company employed 480 local employees, operating 24 hours daily.

The Veterans Building in Guadalupe was established in 1931. It shared the property with the town's volunteer fire and police departments. Seen is a 1951 Maxon fire truck, which was later donated to Hancock College in Santa Maria. (Courtesy of Rancho de Guadalupe Historical Society & Museum.)

In this 1930s photograph, a Guadalupe town parade passes Montoya's Grocery on Guadalupe Street. Other local stores in the 1930s included J. Yamada General Merchandise, Pioneer Meat Market, and Wolfe's Drug Store. (Courtesy of Rancho de Guadalupe Historical Society & Museum.)

From left to right are O.M. Cowden, Jocko Knotts, "Bull" Durham Tognazzini, and Waldo Felts at a Betteravia wildfowl hunt in the 1930s. Union Sugar Company built the community of Betteravia, around its plant. It included housing for plant workers and their families, a store, school, hotel, auditorium, and post office. Although the lake at Betteravia was not suitable for swimming, local residents would often picnic, boat, and hunt fowl around its shoreline.

A 1926 dedication ceremony of a plaque was held at Foxen Canyon, honoring the encampment of American forces there under the command of Lt. Col. John C. Fremont, in 1846. The event was a presentation hosted by the Santa Maria Minerva Club. Standing from left to right are C.L. Preisker, Benton Fremont, Susan E. Lincoln, Michael J. Phillips, and Frank McCoy.

Officially designated as one of the city's historic landmarks on May 16, 1985, the Santa Maria Inn (above) was founded by Irish-born Frank McCoy, who came to Santa Maria in 1904. Located on the outskirts of the downtown area on South Broadway, it was one of the most beautiful and luxurious hotels on the Central Coast. Opening on May 16, 1917, with 24 bedrooms, 24 baths, and a formal dining room (below), it was themed after traditional English inns. Architect Oscar Doane designed the hotel, giving it its English flare. Its popularity and reputation of being an elegant hotel with comfortable accommodations and its ideal location off the main highway between Los Angeles and San Francisco resulted in an expansion to 85 rooms in 1928, and it became the choice place to stay among the elite and celebrity visitors from around the world.

In one of the oldest school districts in the state, Santa Maria High School was founded in 1893. Originally located on the corner of Broadway and Morrison Street, it was demolished in 1921. By 1925, a new Mission Revival–style school was completed. A 100-foot bell tower was connected to both the administration building and the Ethel Pope Auditorium. However, the tower had to be removed in 1963 to comply with state earthquake requirements.

Established in 1931, the Mission Revival–style El Camino School in Santa Maria was one of many buildings designed by valley resident Louis Noire Crawford. Today, El Camino is one of three middle schools in Santa Maria.

Built in 1934, the Mission Revival–style Santa Maria City Hall was designed by Louis Noire Crawford and Francis Parsons. Its intricate and subtle etching designs depict early Spanish history in the valley. The building was featured in the April 1, 1940, issue of *Life* magazine. The city's first mayor was Alvin Cox.

Founded in 1850, the Santa Barbara County Sheriff's Department is one of the oldest law-enforcement agencies in the state. Pictured is a 1935 photograph of Santa Maria's law enforcers. From left to right are Antone Silveria, Paul W. Bovee, Carl T. Monroe (jailer), Tom C. Gullifer, James Brewer, John L. Bishop, Wilbur C. Bartholomew, Ray B. Romero, Deane Laughlin, unidentified, and John D. Ross (undersheriff).

The first Chevrolet dealership was operated by W.B. Johnson and was located in the Houk Building, seen here in the late 1930s. The history of Santa Maria's automotive retail includes Bob Nolan, a service station operator, who signed a Packard franchise agreement and opened Bob Nolan Packard, one of the first dealerships in the city. In the 1920s, Billie Burkhart opened a Pontiac dealership, which later changed to Burkhart Studebaker. In the 1920s, Roemer and Roemer dealt with different car lines, such as Studebaker, Hupmobile, Dort, Briscoe, and King. In the late 1930s, Frank Roemer was the first Buick dealer in the valley. Also opening in the 1930s were Bower Stokes Ford and Ruble Motor Company. In the 1940s, Hollis Terry opened the Chrysler/Plymouth dealership that later became Bell Desoto Plymouth. By the mid-1960s, Bob Nolan was selling Datsuns and Volvos.

Two

THE GREEN VALLEY
WORLD-FAMOUS FLOWER SEEDS, STRAWBERRIES, AND PRODUCE

Lionel Waller, more commonly known as L.D. Waller, was a native of London and skilled in raising flower seeds. In 1912, he founded the Waller Seed Company in Guadalupe. Shortly after the company opened, Dr. John Franklin, who was interested in horticulture, and Paul Giacommi became partners. The company's name changed to Waller Franklin Seed Company. For decades, the seed company continued to ship its award-winning sweet peas, nasturtiums, marigolds, and other flower seeds, as well as vegetable seeds, across the country and worldwide. The company became known around the globe for its choice seeds. Employing many Japanese immigrants to work in the flower fields until their relocation to internment camps, the company later rehired those who returned to the valley after World War II.

When advanced development in irrigation was implemented, agriculture in the valley boomed. By the early 1900s, the Japanese gradually replaced the Chinese in the sugar beet fields, and the labor force doubled. By 1910, a cooperative called the Guadalupe Japanese Association, which supported Japanese farm operations and had a branch in Santa Maria, helped turn the agricultural communities into commercial centers. Japanese immigrant Setsuo Aratani, who arrived in Guadalupe around 1917, began to experiment in growing vegetables and developed a means to ship them to other states, thereby pioneering the vegetable industry in the valley. With the concerted help of the newly formed Guadalupe Japanese Association, Aratani was instrumental in organizing the Guadalupe Produce Company, Guadalupe's first packing plant, and the All Star Trading Company, which imported fertilizer and sake from Japan in 1936. Unfortunately, all of the Aratani properties in Guadalupe were lost during the Japanese internment period—except for the All Star Trading Company, which reopened and continued its operations for decades.

L.D. Waller is pictured at one of the company's marigold fields in the 1930s. Initially planting on 30 acres, he later expanded to more than 350 acres because of the increasing demand for the company's exceptional flower and vegetable seeds, with sweet peas, nasturtiums, and marigolds being the most popular and the bulk of the business.

Acres of marigold rows are shown at one of the Waller Franklin Seed Company's flower fields in Guadalupe.

This c. 1935 photograph is of the Miyoshi family, one of many Japanese families who farmed in the valley. From left to right are "Grandfather," Jun, Riichi (father), Susuma, Akira, Masa (mother), Grace Haruki, and Lena Ogawa. Another family, the Minamis began farming 80 acres in Guadalupe in the 1930s. When Pearl Harbor was bombed in 1941, both H. Yaemon Minami and his older son Yataro were taken away and shuffled among different internment camps all over the West for five years. Upon their return, they were able to retrieve their 80 acres that the bank had held in trust through the years. They began growing cauliflower in 1921, lettuce in 1922, and broccoli in 1924. As a result of an exceptional crop year in 1949, the Minami family expanded their farm of 80 acres to 2,000 acres, which grew to be one of the largest and best-known farms in the state. Yataro is quoted as saying "coming from Japan, where land is so limited, gave us a respect for the land and its use . . . make every acre count, every inch of land."

A mid-1900s photograph shows a water well in Guadalupe, designed and drilled by the Layne & Bowler Pump Company of Los Angeles. A small-diameter pump was placed down the well into the water and connected to a long, vertical shaft at the surface, utilizing a pulley that provided power to extract water. Better irrigation methods greatly increased agricultural production and enabled the area's farms and dairies to flourish.

Rows of broccoli in Guadalupe are shown in the early 1940s. Beginning with only a handful of seeds, Toyokichi Tomooka, one of the organizers of the Santa Maria Produce firm, introduced broccoli to the area. As this was a new vegetable to California, he first planted only four acres. It grew well in the valley and soon became a big-selling crop, which created another boom in the local vegetable industry. (Courtesy of Rancho de Guadalupe Historical Society & Museum.)

Above is an aerial view of 720 acres with a lake in Betteravia, which was a community built around the Union Sugar Company, established in 1897. The advent of Union Sugar increased sugar beet farming and helped it become a cash crop that provided steady income to local farmers. When the Pacific Coast Railway built a spur to the plant site (below), the population of Betteravia grew to approximately 500. Another source that bolstered the area's economy was Union Sugar's waste pulp, which was sold as cattle feed. Howard Brown and Silas Sinton purchased the waste pulp and established the Sinton and Brown Company, which was the first cattle feedlot in Santa Maria and later became one of the country's largest.

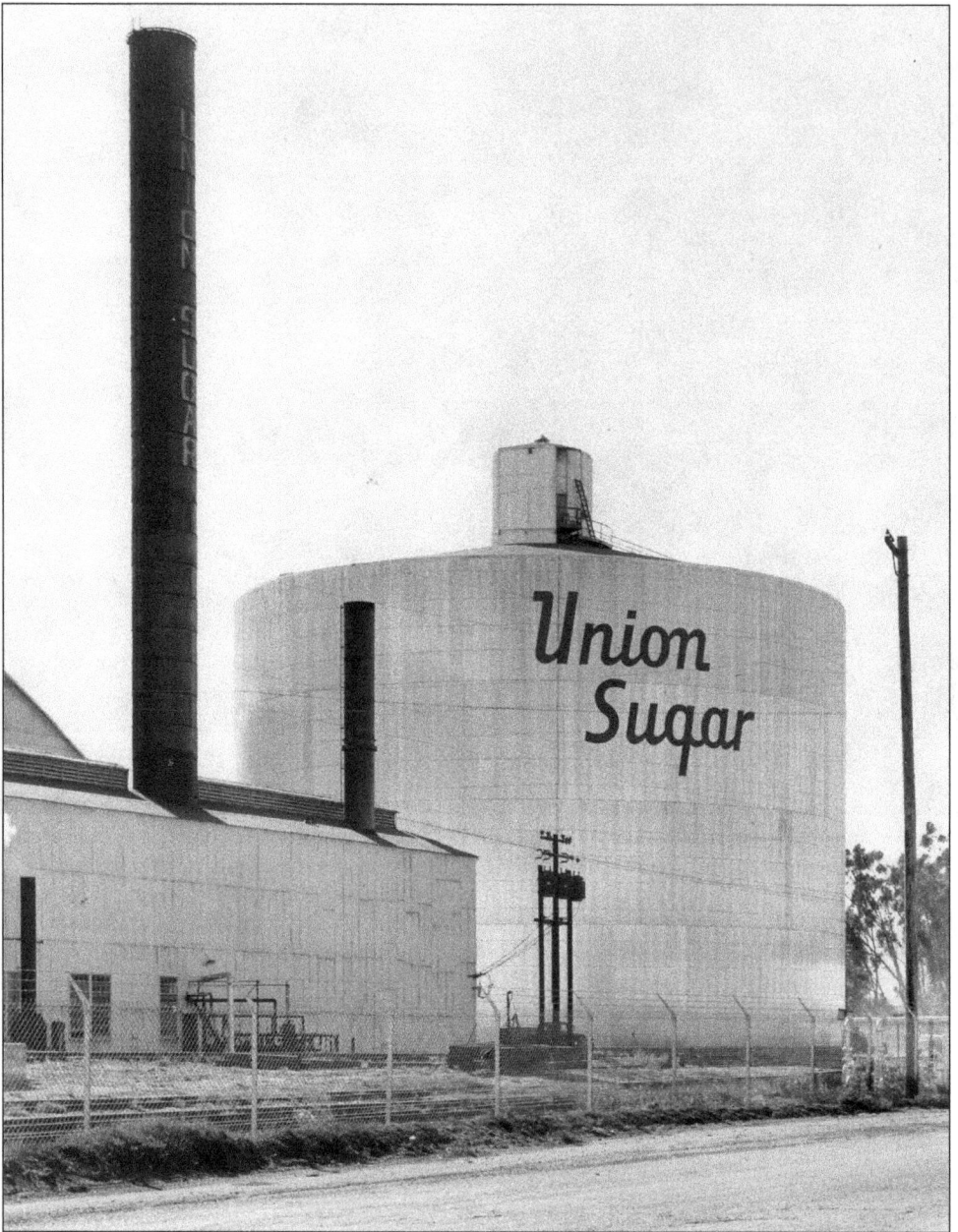

Union Sugar of Betteravia was incorporated in September 1897 by a union of farmers from San Luis Obispo and Santa Barbara Counties who all had a need to get their sugar beets processed. Considered to be a new giant in the valley, the company significantly boosted the local economy by providing jobs and buying locally farmed sugar beets. It contributed millions of tons of beet sugar allotted to the US sugar industry, which is regulated by the federal government, and despite the Depression in the 1930s, market fluctuation, and war, Union Sugar produced beet sugar for more than 30 percent of the nation's sugar needs, for both direct consumption and other food-related products. The company was a division of Consolidated Foods Corporation, which later became a division of Sara Lee Corporation. In 1986, it became Holly Sugar, but the new company did not achieve the success of its predecessor, resulting in lost jobs and plant closure in 1996.

A Union Sugar employee manages newly arrived beets (above). The beets are first dropped into giant water flumes that carry them into the plant, where they are then loaded on a conveyor belt leading to special diffuser machines that force the sugar from the beets. Vacuum pans then evaporate the water from the purified and filtered raw syrup. Centrifuges separate the sugar crystals, which are then bagged and ready for shipment (right).

This photograph shows a field-worker tossing handpicked broccoli into the wagon for delivery to the packinghouse, where it was boxed and kept cool or iced at Rosemary Packing Company, until ready for transport. Lettuce was often packed in boxes and sealed right at the fields. Other local growers and packers included Security Farms & H.Y. Minami & Sons, Tani Farms, and Tomooka Bros., among many others.

Several field-workers harvest celery in Santa Maria in the 1950s. Celery typically requires five to six months to mature. Harvesting begins in July and runs into December. Harvested celery is given a cold-water shower at the packing plant to cool it. After it is cooled, it is packed and stored in a cooler until it is ready for transport.

An unidentified Filipino field-worker is shown in a Guadalupe cauliflower field in the 1950s. In response to America's growing agriculture needs, many young, single Filipino men were first recruited to work the sugarcane fields in Hawaii during the early 1900s. However, harsh working conditions and low wages caused many workers to leave Hawaii and seek jobs in California, where they followed crop seasons that kept them employed through most of the year. Although plentiful work was to be found in California, it was not without problems. With a fast-growing agricultural industry, California growers were in need of more field-workers, which, in turn, created a need for structure and organization in wages and working conditions. In 1962, the United Farm Workers of America, a labor union initially created from the efforts of Filipino and Mexican organizers (Larry Itliong and Cesar Chavez, respectively), was founded to help workers obtain unemployment insurance. It soon became a union of farmworkers. However, on August 21, 1975, a gathering of union organizers, talking to field-workers at Koyama Farms in Guadalupe, resulted in a violent attack by members of the Teamsters Union.

A 1950s photograph shows a farmworker in a Guadalupe carrot field stacking harvested carrots along a row to be picked up and brought to the plant for cooling and packaging.

Farmworkers in Guadalupe in the 1970s are harvesting and packing lettuce directly into boxes for the Obispo Packing Company. (Courtesy of Santa Maria Elks Lodge 1538 History Committee.)

Pictured is a 1930s pea crop camp near Nipomo, a community close to Guadalupe. Several tents dot a cleared area between rolling hills. Field-workers and their families lived in the temporary housing tents during the crop season.

In the late 1940s, four women work on an apparatus used to plant strawberry seedlings on a strawberry farm in Santa Maria. The harvesting of strawberries is very labor-intensive because the berries are delicate, and they must be handled carefully.

Produce broker Edward J. Pryor (left) and an unidentified Sheehy employee supervise the loading of strawberries for shipment to eastern markets. Once harvested, strawberries must be precooled, packed in precooled packaging, and shipped under refrigeration to arrive on the Eastern Seaboard with less than two-percent spoilage.

Commercially grown strawberries have been the valley's top crop for the past several decades, with several farms throughout the valley comprising more than 7,000 acres dedicated to growing strawberries. Pictured are Robert Sheehy (left) and Terry Sheehy, holding a case of locally grown strawberries from the Sheehy Farms.

A 1947 photograph shows the *Flying Tiger*, the first aircraft used to transport strawberries from the Sheehy Farms out of Santa Maria. Its first destination was Chicago, Illinois. Kenneth T. Sheehy (left) and son Robert Sheehy are pictured with the airplane.

The Sheehys were the first family that began commercial strawberry farming in the valley. Kenneth and his brother Rod Sheehy partnered with Ned Driscoll and Tom Porter to form the valley's first commercial strawberry operation in 1944.

Workers at the Polly Pak Company in Santa Maria carefully box Field Gold brand carrots in this 1956 photograph.

Sitting ready for loading and transport of strawberries are seven Sheehy Berry Farm trucks in Santa Maria. The truck at right in this 1950s photograph is almost fully loaded.

A young boy carrying two buckets of eggs was an advertisement for Rosemary Farm. Founded by Capt. G. Allan Hancock in 1925, the farm was named after his daughter Rosemary. The egg farm gained national attention in the 1980s for its introduction of low-cholesterol, low-sodium eggs. Selling mainly to local areas, it annually produced, from a flock of about 300,000 chickens, approximately 75 million eggs, 50,000 of which were brown, fertile eggs sold to health food stores.

Allan Hancock's efforts in improving agricultural methods greatly contributed to the continued development of crop irrigation, soil analysis, fertilization, packing, and shipping, and the growth of an ice and cold-storage company to pack and ship produce. Shown here is an unidentified Rosemary Farm employee displaying freshly harvested lettuce.

Harvesting in the late 1800s and into the early 1900s was more laborious than in later years because of the lack of advanced farming equipment, portable bathroom facilities, and readily available drinking water. In this photograph, a young child (lower left) and three adults (lower right) carrying baskets and several field-workers harvesting peas in Santa Maria can be seen.

Field-workers are shown picking lettuce for Security Farms in Guadalupe in the early 1940s.

Three

SPORTS
MAJOR LEAGUES AND THE OLYMPICS

When baseball was introduced to the valley in 1882, it soon became the most popular game played locally. Fields were cleared, and teams began to form, especially in 1904, after the discovery of oil in Orcutt. Every oil lease company supported a local baseball team; other teams were sponsored by various businesses, organizations, and schools. The fun, competition, and community gatherings that the sport attracted made baseball a staple of recreation in the Santa Maria Valley. The Santa Maria Indians Baseball Club was founded in 1944 and is one of the oldest semiprofessional baseball teams in the country. It was one of two teams to win the National Baseball Congress Tournament in Wichita, Kansas. From the club emerged athletes such as Jackie Jensen, Jim Lonborg, Mike Aldrete, Robin Ventura, and Ozzie Smith, who went on to play in major leagues. Setsuo Aratani, from Guadalupe, was a baseball enthusiast, and in 1928, he sponsored a team to compete in Japan. Football and basketball were also popular sports, with each local school having its own teams, and two Santa Maria star swimmers participated in Summer Olympics, one in Los Angeles in 1932 and the other in Rome in 1960. Other local notables who had distinguished themselves throughout the years were inducted into Guadalupe's Sports Hall of Fame on May 29, 2004. Inductees included Rodrigo Abajado, Tony and Frank Almaguer, Fred Amido, George Aratani, Mickey Bernardo, Ron Estabello, Jim Gamble, Leo Gondalfi, Alfredo Gutierrez, Leo B. Julian, Max Kitagawa, John Lizalde, Dick Maretti, Johnny Martinez, and Frank Montez Sr.

This late-1800s Santa Maria men's baseball team was one of many local squads to form since baseball was introduced to the valley in 1882. From left to right are (first row) Charles Arrelanes, Jim Davidson, and Herschel Miller; (second row) Dave Arellanes, John Arellanes, and Bill Miller; (third row) Bert Blosser, Ike Miller, Harry Saulsbury, Joe Fisher, and Haight Jesse.

The 1909 Santa Maria Golden Bears are pictured. They are, from left to right, (first row) Bert Jessee, Lee Brown, Nelson Jones, and Mac Langlor; (second row) Landon Bagly, Elwood Bryant, Emmett Trott, Fred Haslam (in derby), Archie Cline, Elmer Boyd, Dick Doans, and Bert Smith.

Shown is a 1936 Santa Maria Mendocino Wines baseball team. Pictured are, from left to right, (first row) George Hobbs, unidentified, John Brumana, Charles Howard (young child), Art Pimental, Roy Metler, and Harry Saunders; (second row) Pete Brumana, Marshall Brumana, Frank Brumana, Red McDermont, Charles Howard, Rolland Levey, and ? Horn.

Pictured at bottom center, between two Santa Maria Shriners, is a young Santa Maria Little League member wearing an Indians uniform at a 1950s Indians game. In 1950, Bill Ellis, Harry Goodchild, Butch Simas, Larry Lavagnino, Carl Barbettini, and others brought Little League baseball to Santa Maria. The first teams included Associated Drug's Dodgers, Casey's Orcutt Tigers, Coca-Cola Little Cokes, Union Sugar, Melby's Jewelers, and Peterson Auto Parts.

This is a 1907 photograph of a Santa Maria High School boys' basketball team.

A Santa Maria Union High School baseball team is shown in the late 1800s. From left to right are (first row) Elwood Bryant and unidentified; (second row) Roy Tunnell, Stanley McFaddin, and unidentified; (third row) unidentified, unidentified, Harold Stonier, Chester Martin, and unidentified.

The Santa Maria Union High School girls' basketball team appears in 1906. Pictured from left to right are Gertrude Smith, Ora Harris, Olga Kortner, Alfa Jones, Teresa McDonald, and Litti Paulding. The girls formed a club called TBDL Club, which stood for, "to be determined later."

Shown is an Orcutt School boys' basketball team in 1950.

This is a Santa Maria Union High School's 1940s football team. From left to right are Nello Del Porto, ? Tudor, ? Buzzini, Chuck Taylor, Louie Grabil, Bill Saunders, and "Lardo" Marion Smith.

Santa Maria Union High School's 1920 basketball team photograph includes, from left to right, (first row) Howard Evans, Douglas Smith, and Ernie Righetti; (second row) Dan Currryer and coach Louis Crawford; (third row) Wilfred Rutherford, Kenneth Kennedy, Raymond Strong, and Darrel Patterson.

This is a Santa Maria Golden Dukes basketball team in the 1950s. Champions of the Santa Maria City Basketball League in 1947–1948, they were members of the amateur National Industrial Basketball League for five years, beginning early in the 1950s, and played for five years. Home games were played in the old Armory Building at the Santa Maria Fairpark. Pictured are, from left to right, (first row) Quentin Sims, Ken Milo, Joe White, Omer Meeker, Gus Richer, and Bill Birka; (second row) manager Duke Webster, Bob McCutcheon, Sherman Nearman, Madison Stanford, Vern Barton, Jim Segrue, Will Daley, and coach "Hop" Findlay. (Courtesy of Bob McCutcheon.)

Johnny Paulson (left) and actor Buster Crabbe are pictured in 1933. John Paulson, Santa Maria High School class of 1933, was captain of Santa Maria High School's swimming team for four years. He was the first local to compete in a Summer Olympics, in Los Angeles in 1932.

The Santa Maria Municipal Plunge, on South Broadway, was the original site of the town's first waterworks building, founded by Rueben Hart in 1916. In 1920, it was converted to a 20-yard pool and became Santa Maria's first public swimming pool. In 1926, Paul Nelson took over the management of the Plunge and trained Johnny Paulsen, the Santa Marian who participated in the 1932 Summer Olympics.

Pictured is a 1928 swim meet at the Plunge. Standing in front at right (from left to right) are Paul Nelson, Cassius Perkiss, and Dorwin Coy. Nelson encouraged Eugene Lenz to try out for the Santa Maria swim team. Lenz excelled at swimming and later became the second Santa Marian to participate in a Summer Olympics, in Rome in 1960.

Four

COMMUNITY SPIRIT
PATRIOTISM, CLUBS,
AND ORGANIZATIONS

On August 14, 1918, residents of the city of Santa Maria came together for the dedication of the city's new 100-foot flagpole. The ceremony was held downtown, and the flagpole was erected in the center of Main Street and Broadway. Under the American flag was raised a service flag, bearing a star that represented each serviceman from Santa Maria. Under the service flag, smaller flags of America's allies were raised. The outcome of the community coming together to plan the 1918 event, from the flagpole's design and construction to its financing, evidenced the unity of the community. The early clubs and organizations established in the valley, many of which are still in existence today, were all founded in the spirit of helping others. These early groups and organizations include Masonic and Odd Fellows lodges, Elks Lodge 1538, Knights of Pythias, Rotary International, Lions International, Kiwanis, Moose Chapter 463, Pioneer Association, Fraternal Order of Eagles (FOE), Altrusa International, and the Grand Army of the Republic (GAR), to name only a few. Each has contributed to the growth, development, and well-being of the community in general and of its youth, in particular.

Preparing for the "Barbecue" at Betteravia, Cal.
Aston-Photo-no 848

The traditional Santa Maria barbecue has its roots dating back to Spanish California, when family, friends, and neighbors would gather at a rancho to feast on meat cooked over local red-oak coals. Pictured are early residents of the Betteravia community in the early 1900s, gathered for a Santa Maria–style barbecue of meats cooked in an earthen pit.

A Santa Maria Elks Lodge member tends to a large rack of top-block sirloin roasts on skewers at a 1960s local event. Meat used in a Santa Maria–style barbecue is not limited to the tri-tip cut of beef that is more popularly known today. Tri-tip's debut came in the late 1950s, when large beef loins were cut into sections that left triangular shaped pieces. Those cutaway pieces became tri-tip. (Courtesy of Elks Lodge 1538 Historical Department.)

Elks Lodge members barbecue several skewers of top block at a 1960s lodge event. Santa Maria–style barbecue is not served with sauce. It is simply seasoned with salt, garlic salt, and pepper and is traditionally served with pinquito beans (grown only in Santa Maria), fresh salad (made with lettuce from local farms), fresh homemade salsa, and buttered bread, typically sourdough that is warmed on the grill. (Courtesy of Elks Lodge 1538 Historical Department.)

Members of the Santa Maria Shriners ready for a ceremonial event in 1940. The club's barbecue team prepares to cook the meal. In the background is the rear of Santa Maria High School.

On August 14, 1918, residents of Santa Maria come together for the dedication of the city's 100-foot flagpole, in honor of local men and women serving in the military during World War I. The dedication was held downtown, and the flagpole was erected in the center of the intersection of Main Street and Broadway. Below the American flag, a service flag bearing a star that represented each serviceman from Santa Maria was raised.

Santa Maria celebrates Armistice Day on November 11, 1920. The streets are crowded with military men and women, who had returned home from the war. A platform is seen in front of the Bradley Hotel.

Founded in 1920, the A to Z Club celebrated its 30th anniversary at the Santa Maria Inn on February 16, 1950. The club provided anonymous charitable acts to the local needy. Pictured from left to right are (first row) Rebecca Wineman, Mrs. James MacDonald, Lucille Conrad, Rosemary Engel, Norma Goodbrod, and Mildred McCullers; (second row) Edwina Twitchell, Pauline Adam, Marie Lepping, Betty Sherrill, Eileen Stone, Elizabeth Rubel, Mary Bertero, Leila Hughes, Helen Missell, Katherine Donovan, and Dorothy Ford.

A Santa Maria Chamber of Commerce meeting at the US Grill is pictured on January 25, 1921. Founded in 1906, the chamber held its meetings in a small office on the corner of South Lincoln and West Church Streets for several years, and it later occupied an office in city hall. It is now permanently located on South Broadway. Its mission is to "maintain the economy and improve and increase business and growth in Santa Maria."

Pictured are Women of the Moose in 1924. Originally called Women of Mooseheart, Women of the Moose became an auxiliary in 1913. It is part of the Loyal Order of Moose, which was established in the late 1800s and was originally a fraternal organization. During the first decade of the 20th century, it transformed into an organization for men and women devoted to helping children in need across North America.

Another early fraternal organization, whose "purpose is to make good men better," is the Santa Maria Shriners. Pictured at a 1940s Shriners barbecue event are, from left to right, Gene Martin, Larry Kife, Kenny Trefts, Lou Thompson, Tom Parks, and Ernie Righetti.

Pictured in front of the Rex Café in Santa Maria are contestants who participated in the annual Elks Rodeo Beard-O-Reno event in the late 1940s. Contestants were judged according to the blackest, reddest, best characterization, best mustache, grayest, best sideburns, best goatee, longest, most original, best attempt, and wildest. At right is a sign on a light post indicating the direction of the communities of Betteravia and Guadalupe.

Sponsored by the Kiwanis Club of Santa Maria, the Boy Scouts of America Santa Maria Troop 2 is assembled on the steps of Santa Maria High School's auditorium in 1944. There were many local youth organizations that fostered community involvement and self-development. The 4-H Club taught young adults the dignity of work, skills, cooperation, and responsibility, and its insignia represents head, heart, hands, and health.

In a 1940s parade on Broadway, sponsored by the Kiwanis Club of Santa Maria, the Camp Fire Girls Club and Boy Scouts of America Troop 2 ride on a 1947 stake-bed truck. In tow is an antique car with a bearded man (backseat), baseball player (standing), golfer, and football player (front seat). In the background are a Bank of America, Sears market, and several neighborhood stores.

In June 1952, a parade of antique automobiles was held on Broadway and ended at the fairgrounds. Shown from left to right are a 1905 Maxwell, 1915 Ford, and a Pierce Arrow built between 1901 and 1938. The event was organized by the Horseless Carriage Club of America and attracted a large local crowd.

Shown is a wartime parade in Santa Maria in 1941. Military vehicles proceed down Broadway as residents crowd the streets to show support for servicemen during World War II. Several early stores and businesses can be seen. At left is the Santa Maria News Stand. Across the street are, from left to right, the bell tower of the First United Methodist Church, a hardware, Holser and Bailey, Chop Suey Café, Grayson Hotel, a barbershop, Andrews Grocery, and Gallison's Market.

Fostering family values and youth recreation, the Santa Maria Elks Club held a father-son dinner event for its members and their sons in the 1950s. (Courtesy of Santa Maria Elks Lodge 1538 History Committee.)

The original Knights of Pythias Building housed the county offices and chamber of commerce on the first floor and had complete lodge facilities on the second floor. Its new building, as seen here, was designed by local architect Louis Crawford in the 1940s. One of the town's earliest organizations, the Fraternal Order of Knights of Pythias promotes "cooperation and friendship between people of good will."

Rodeo weekend in Santa Maria is a big annual event. The planning of the next year's event begins shortly after the current year's rodeo weekend ends. Pictured are rodeo supporters in 1944 socializing at the Rex Café, where rodeo tickets for the Elk's second rodeo event were sold. Pictured from left to right are L.P. Scaroni, Jocko Knotts, Al Stone, Rick Ferini, Owen Cowden, and Jim Short. (Courtesy of Santa Maria Elks History Committee.)

A PER (Past Exalted Ruler) and service pin night, awarding 35 years of lodge service, was held on February 17, 1955, at the Santa Maria Elks Lodge 1538. Pictured from left to right are Gorton Miller, Charles T. McDermont, J.S. McDonell, and Herschell Scott. (Courtesy of Santa Maria Elks History Committee.)

Shown is the old Santa Maria Elks Club Lodge 1538, located on Main and Vine Streets. It was demolished in 1975 as part of the new Town Center Mall development. (Courtesy of Santa Maria Elks History Committee.)

This is an aerial view of the Elks Rodeo Grounds. The annual Santa Maria Elks Club Rodeo was founded after the organization created a foundation to raise money for Santa Maria's youth. For decades, the rodeo was held at the fairgrounds, but Union Oil gifted the club with a large tract of land, on the condition that all monies made from events held there would be utilized for the benefit of youth recreation. (Courtesy of Santa Maria Elks History Committee.)

A local cowboy rides a bucking horse at an annual Elks Rodeo in the 1960s. The first Elks rodeo event was held in 1943, during World War II, and featured several local cowboys who competed in bull riding, bareback and saddleback bronco riding, bulldogging, and team calf and steer roping. It cost $5 to enter an event. (Courtesy of Santa Maria Elks History Committee.)

Bulls used in the events were borrowed from neighboring farms. The rodeo grew to become one of the biggest events in the valley, one of the largest rodeos in California, and one of the top rodeo events nationwide. The annual rodeos have raised millions of dollars since their beginning, enabling the club to donate millions of dollars to local youth recreational groups throughout the years. (Courtesy of Santa Maria Elks History Committee.)

Sponsored by the Santa Maria Elks Club as part of its many youth recreation events, a children's rodeo competition event in the 1970s features a young boy wrestling down a sheep. (Courtesy of Santa Maria Elks History Committee.)

Shown is the Santa Maria Elks 13th Annual Rodeo Parade, held on June 2, 1956. Pictured in the wagon are, from left to right, (first row) Clarence Minetti and Andy Jaurequr; (second row) Susie Minetti (child) and Rosalie Minetti; (third row) Russ Griffith and Rick Barret; (fourth row) unidentified and Bill Huddy. (Courtesy of Santa Maria Elks Lodge 1538 History Committee.)

In 1932, Loudon and Eula Gatewood and their eight children became the first black family to settle in Santa Maria. Loudon opened the Gatewood Shine Parlor on South Broadway, between Church and West Main Streets. The parlor thrived during World War II but closed after the war. A new city street sign, Gatewood Way, was created in the family's honor and unveiled at a dedication ceremony held on November 15, 2006.

Five

PLANES AND TRAINS
HISTORIC FLIGHTS AND ONE OF THE
BUSIEST SHORT LINES IN THE COUNTRY

In the 1930s, Capt. G. Allan Hancock established and was president of Santa Maria Farms Co., Rosemary Farm, and Rosemary Packing Company. Hancock's many contributions to Santa Maria are almost equal to the valley's oil boom in the early 1900s and the establishment of Union Sugar; all enabled the town to grow and prosper. His introduction of new irrigation methods helped many farmers, who had previously utilized dry-farming techniques, to expand and prosper in the production of fruits and various crops. In addition, Hancock established the Santa Maria Ice & Cold Storage Company, for the holding and packing of fresh-harvested crops, and the La Brea Securities Company. His innovations in farming also included improvements in dairying, cattle breeding, and egg production. In addition to opening the gates for the valley's agricultural industry, Hancock purchased the Santa Maria Valley Railroad, which was built in 1911 for the transport of oil from the local area and to connect with the Southern Pacific Railroad in Guadalupe. He modernized the Santa Maria Valley Railroad by replacing steam locomotives with diesel-electric trains. This led to an agricultural boom that, in turn, created more local jobs in the planting, harvesting, packing, and transport of fruits and vegetables around the country. Captain Hancock also founded the Hancock College of Aeronautics, which served as a training ground for thousands of pilots. It was one of nine schools across the country providing elementary flight training and aircraft mechanics. Many graduates of the college became World War II fighter pilots. Hancock also financed the historic *Southern Cross* flight across the Pacific Ocean to Australia. His aeronautic interests eventually led to the founding of Santa Maria Airlines. Hancock passed away in 1965.

Good friends Marian Mullin and Bertram Hancock appear in this photograph. Bertram was killed in the Santa Barbara earthquake in 1925, when the floor above him collapsed at the Arlington Hotel in Santa Barbara. Bertram's father, Capt. G. Allan Hancock, later married Marian Mullin in 1946.

This portrait of Capt. G. Allan and Marian Hancock is from the early 1960s.

Capt. G. Allan Hancock appears in front of the historic *Southern Cross* airplane in 1928. It was a high-winged Fokker monoplane with a 71-foot wingspan. Hancock purchased it and funded the flight across the Pacific Ocean, begun on May 31, 1928, by Charles Edward Kingsford Smith, an Australian World War I flying ace, and copilot Capt. Charles T.P. Ulm. Painted bright blue and crowded inside with fuel and supplies, it safely landed in Brisbane, Australia, on June 9.

After completing the historic flight, the *Southern Cross* continued on to London, Ireland, Newfoundland, and New York and then returned to Oakland, California. When the *Southern Cross* landed at Hancock Field, it was greeted by hundreds of Santa Marians.

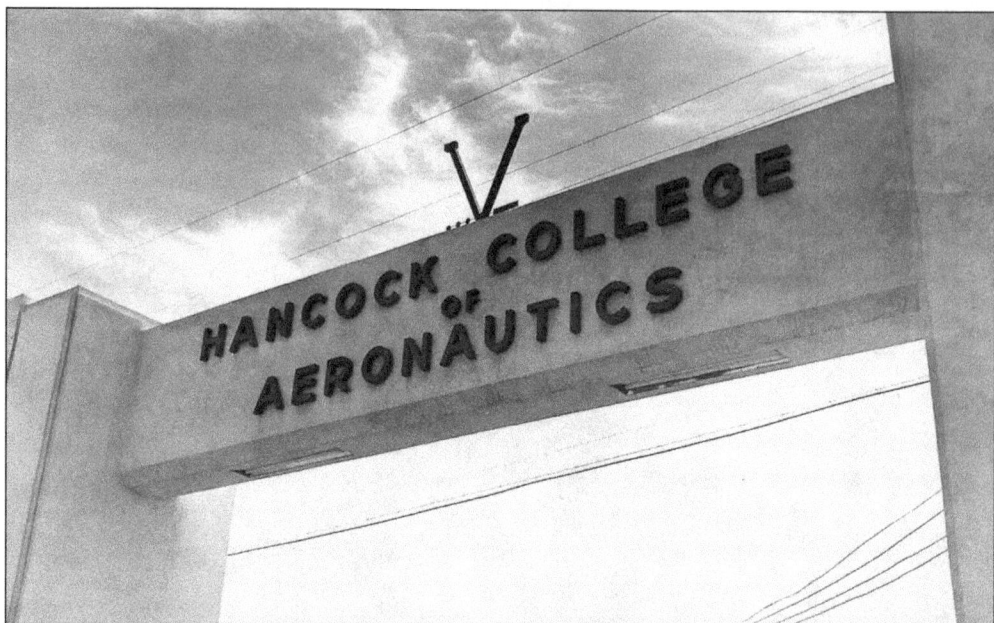

In the 1930s, Capt. G. Allan Hancock transformed Hancock Field into a school for pilots and called it the Hancock College of Aeronautics. He purchased additional land and built a runway, hangars, a dormitory, and classrooms. The school trained and prepped many pilots in both aviation and aviation mechanics. It became one of the nation's first privately owned schools for pilots. Many graduates entered into the military flying program at nearby Santa Maria Army Air Base.

Student pilots attend class in one of several classrooms built at the aeronautic school in the 1930s.

The current location of the Santa
Maria Airport was once Santa Maria
Army Air Base, also a training facility
for B-25 bombers and P-38 fighters,
as seen here in the 1940s. The
overwhelming presence of military
in the area not only transformed the
town into a loud and bustling military
environment, but it also boosted
the economy with jobs in Santa
Maria and at nearby Camp Cooke,
now Vandenberg Air Force Base.

Posing next to one of the school's
PT-22s in the 1930s are five
graduates of the Hancock College of
Aeronautics. Although the school
was affordable, costing $4,500 to
complete the program, compared to
the government's cost of $25,000 to
train a pilot, the Great Depression
caused it to close in 1934, but it
reopened in 1939. After World War
II, Santa Maria Community College
occupied the school and changed
its name to Allan Hancock College,
in honor of Captain Hancock.

The main training plane used at Hancock College of Aeronautics was the PT-22, but the school also used PT-17s, Steirmans, Ryans, Fairchild PT-19s, Cessna twin-engine planes (known as Bamboo Bombers), PT-26s, DC-3s, and the B-13 (known as the old Vultee Vibrator). Standing next to a PT-22 in the early 1930s are, from left to right, instructor Leon Durden and students Thomas V. Gray, Sam Handren, Richard E. Cartier, Earl L. ?, and George W. Antis.

Capt. G. Allan Hancock, second from left, his wife, Marian, and others review plans to expand Hancock Field to include a larger runway, hangars, dormitory, and classrooms for Hancock College of Aeronautics in the 1930s.

The Pacific Coast Railway station was located on West Main Street. The train seen here is in front of the Hart House on East Main Street. It was an electric locomotive that pulled wooden coaches that carried passengers and freight along Main Street and to Guadalupe. In Guadalupe, the railroad connected with the Southern Pacific Railroad, which ran between San Francisco and Los Angeles.

In 1925, a christening event was held for the new locomotive of the Santa Maria Valley Railroad, seen here in front of the Security First National Bank. The locomotive pulled 10 flatcars. Of those, nine were for cargo, and the last was equipped with benches and railings for passengers. Railroads filled an important role in the development of the Central Coast by hauling cargo, such as lumber from ships, as well as providing shipment of goods and services from distant cities.

The Santa Maria Valley Railroad depot is shown in the 1940s. In the background can be seen the Santa Maria Ice & Cold Storage Company. At right is a passenger car with the name "Arizona and New Mexico" on its side.

Shown is a Santa Maria Valley Railroad beet train on the unloading trestle at the Union Sugar Company plant in Betteravia around 1905.

Capt. G. Allan Hancock (middle) purchased the Santa Maria Valley Railroad in 1925. Improvements included the addition of rails and the replacement of nine steam locomotives with diesel-electric engines. His La Brea Ice Plant and the 400-acre Rosemary Farm was located along the right-of-way, which enabled convenient loading and unloading of products onto the trains. The Santa Maria Valley Railroad connected with the Southern Pacific Railroad, which enabled products and produce to be sent to markets around the world.

Pictured is one of the modern diesel-electric locomotives. Traveling 30 miles of rail, the Santa Maria Valley Railroad became one of the busiest short lines in the country.

A 1950s photograph shows two cattle buyers at the Sinton and Brown feed lot in Santa Maria.

A Southern Pacific train filled with sugar beets passes through Gaviota in mid-Santa Barbara County in the 1930s. It is bound for the Santa Maria Valley to deliver its load to the Union Sugar plant in Betteravia. Although many local farmers in and around the valley were growing sugar beets as a cash crop, their output was not enough to supply Union Sugar's needs.

Six

REFLECTIONS
LOOKING BACK OVER THE YEARS

Although the Santa Maria Valley was primarily an agriculture community, the city was no different than most growing municipalities in the country. By the 1950s, recreational facilities, restaurants, movie theaters, and many new businesses were established around the valley. Downtown stores and businesses lit up the night with neon lights, and young people cruised Broadway while listening to radio station KSEE-AM and danced at the Veterans Hall. Waller Park once had a zoo, and the Paul Nelson pool opened. The city's multiethnic community offered a variety of eateries, including Joe's Mexicatessen, Chop Suey Café, A&W, Maestros, Bernies, Frederick's Pizza, Chew Café, Quitos, Foster Freeze, B&B Café, Pappys, Jumbo's restaurant (on South Broadway), the Boy's restaurant (on East Main), and Merrell's Steak House (also on East Main Street).

To see a movie, residents could visit the Highway Drive-in, Park Aire Drive-in, Santa Maria Theater, and the Gaiety Theater. Visitors stayed at the Santa Maria Inn, Sundown Motel, Capri Motel, Massy Hotel, and the Valley Motel, to name a few. Neighborhood markets included Purity Market, Scolaris, and J.J.'s. Shopping Centers included a variety of stores, such as Peggy's Fashions, McMahan's furniture, and Love Lace dress shop. The Oak Knolls Village shopping center hosted a pharmacy, the Cornet store, and the Tan Top bakery. The Town Center Mall opened in July 1977. It was the first two-story, enclosed shopping center in the area. It first had two department store anchors, Sears and Gottschalk's, and soon grew to host 85 additional retailers. It became the focus of the Central Coast for shopping. Locals will always remember Haslam's, Joey's Market, Parsons Bros., Rexall Drugs, Paramount Cleaners-Laundry, Longs Drugs, Conrad Drugs, Bellis Drugs, Kalton's Pet-Land, Blosser's Hotel, and JC Penney at the Santa Maria shopping center. In the late 1950s, the Stowell Shopping Center opened; it had several eateries and businesses, including the Pearl East restaurant, Armed Forces Recruit Center, Book Nook, Ice Cream Social, A-One Barber Shop, Baldwin Music, the Coachman, and Bill and Nick's Liquors, among many others. This was the town of Santa Maria, and these were some of the places that will always be remembered.

On September 11, 1955, Mayor Leonard S. Petersen buries a time capsule in city hall's courtyard during the city's 50th anniversary celebration of Santa Maria's incorporation.

A large crowd of community members gathers at city hall during a war bond rally in the early 1940s. A flagpole was erected during World War I that was originally located in the middle of the intersection of Broadway and Main Street in 1918, but it was later moved to the city hall grounds to protect it from damage from heavy military traffic that crossed the intersection during World War II.

Associated Gasoline station and the Santa Maria Auto Court are pictured in the 1920s. The automobile court sign reads, "All cabins have hot showers & toilets, linens & blankets." It was located in the 900 block of North Broadway. (Courtesy of Santa Maria Elks Lodge History Committee.)

Standing next to the gasoline pumps is believed to be Hugh Bacon, manager of Mission Service Station in the 1930s. The station was located in Guadalupe, at the corner of what are now Tenth and Guadalupe Streets. It later became a Union 76 station and was destroyed in a 1990 explosion. A second station in town was the Sun Rise, owned by Y. Oishi Company. (Courtesy of Rancho de Guadalupe Historical Society & Museum.)

Established Since 1918

U.S. GRILL

U.S. Grill   U.S. Grill

SPECIALIZING IN SEA FOODS AND JUICY STEAKS

180 Miles to Los Angeles ✦ SANTA MARIA, CALIFORNIA on the Coast Highway ✦ 262 Miles to San Francisco

The U.S. Grill was a popular Santa Maria restaurant in the early 1900s that specialized in seafood and steaks. Its Mission Revival–style building, with a tiled clay roof and arched windows, resembled a modern adobe.

Established in 1931, the Guadalupe Veterans Memorial Building is pictured in the 1960s. The Guadalupe Police Department and the volunteer fire department shared the same grounds at the rear of the building. (Courtesy of Santa Maria Elks Lodge History Committee.)

A young woman can be seen beside one of several early-1940s-model American cars parked in front of F.W. Woolworth Co., in the Gibson-Drexler Building. The building's original brick-bearing walls were replaced with steel columns. On the second floor were the offices of dentist Dr. E.K. Dart and chiropractor Dr. L.M. Clemons. To the left of Woolworth's are Ze Dail and Gardner-Wheaton Drugs.

Dating back to the Central City days, residents purchased their harnesses, buggy whips, Nu-Back corsets, children's underwear, and men's work clothes from the Sears catalog. Sears came to Santa Maria in 1939, and its big sellers at the time were Lux soap flakes, lace curtains, swoop brimmed hats, and replacement parts for Ford Model Ts. Through the years, the store moved—from Bradley Road and Cypress Street to Church Street, and later to the Town Center Mall.

A popular hangout for young locals was Leo's drive-in restaurant. Dancing at the Veterans Hall, cruising Broadway on Friday and Saturday nights, and meeting at Leo's drive-in for hamburgers, fries, and shakes were the popular things for young people to do in the 1950s and 1960s.

Larry's Western Shop on Broadway sold saddles, riding accessories, hats, and Western wear. In the window are advertisements urging customers to vote for 1966–1967 queen candidate Linda Lemus, from Guadalupe. Other queen candidates for the 23rd annual Elks Rodeo and Parade were Linda Nielsen, Norma Graham, Rosie Medina, Jama Newland, Debby Sinsabaugh, and Kay York. Linda Lemus won first place. The contest raised $48,789.

Another popular hangout for young locals was Rick's drive-in restaurant, established in the 1940s and located at North Broadway and Donovan Road.

Rick's drive-in restaurant also had an inside dining area that was decorated in old-country style, with wooden tables, pieces of antique furniture and other antiques, including a spinning wheel. It was known for its pies and strawberry shortcake, which were served year-round.

At the Weber's bakery plant in Santa Maria, seven unidentified employees pose in this 1950s photograph next to one of Weber's bread-delivery trucks.

The neighborhood G&F Market (Gallison's & Felmlee) is pictured in the 1950s. Knudsen and Flav-R-Pack delivery trucks are parked in front of the store. The First Methodist Church bell tower can be seen in the background.

Glenn Roemer Hardware is pictured in the 1960s. Skilled mechanic and tradesman Joseph Roemer arrived in Santa Maria in the late 1800s from Austria. In addition to blacksmithing, Glenn built the framework for bean-cutting and many tools associated with farming and often took eggs or potatoes as payment. He later diversified into woodworking and welding. Joseph built some of the first buses used by Santa Maria Union High School, which was founded in 1893.

Shown is Rick's Rancho drive-in and eat-in restaurant. Later, Rick's Rancho expanded to include a motel with a swimming pool and restaurant.

Established in 1936 by Arnold Melby as a watchmaker store on North Broadway in Santa Maria, Melby's later began selling jewelry. In 1945, Arnold's son Donald came into the business; he sold the North Broadway store in 1946 and opened one on West Main Street. In 1950, the store expanded to add 1,000 square feet, which became the sterling silver room. In 1960, the business expanded again with an additional 2,000 square feet, which became the gift shop.

The Oriental Gift Shop on Broadway is pictured in the 1960s. Next door is the Restwell Motel that offered kitchenettes in each of its rooms.

Founded by Joe Scolari in 1948, Scolari's Supermarket first opened in Old Town Orcutt and later followed with a series of chains around the Central Coast. The stores were sold to Lucky Stores in the mid-1970s, but a few of the smaller store buildings were kept. One of the smaller locations was the original store and became J.J.'s and, later, the Old Town Market in Orcutt. (Courtesy of Mark Steller, Old Town Market.)

Williams Bros. Market was a family-owned, Santa Maria–based chain that had 19 stores located from Santa Barbara to Morro Bay, with several stores in Santa Maria. Pictured here in the 1950s is the first market, located on East Church Street. The chain was sold to Vons Cos. in the 1990s.

The first Garden Dairy was located at 219 East Main Street and owned by Dick Armstrong. Later, a drive-thru Garden Dairy (seen here) opened in the valley. Its milk was bottled in tall, round, pyro-glazed one-gallon bottles and also came in smaller sizes.

Farmers Market, located on North Broadway, is pictured in the 1950s. Locally grown fruits and vegetables were sold outside the store in bins.

Opened in 1954 on Broadway, the Swiss Chalet was a favorite dine-in restaurant popular for its rotisserie chicken and barbecued meats, especially the porterhouse steak for two.

Shaw's Restaurant is another favorite dine-in restaurant, popular for its barbecued meats that are cooked behind a viewing window so patrons can watch. It has been a longtime favorite gathering place for dinner, cocktails, and meetings. (Courtesy of Eric Spies.)

Established in 1960, Rancho Bowl, located on East Donovan Road near Broadway, has been a longtime favorite bowling alley.

Thrifty Drug store, located on South Broadway in the 1960s, was a favorite place to go for ice cream.

Simas Sporting Goods store, located on East Main Street, is pictured in the 1950s. The store sold sporting equipment, from surfboards to bicycles. It was founded by Leland J. "Butch" Simas, who operated the business for many years. His son Bill later took over its management.

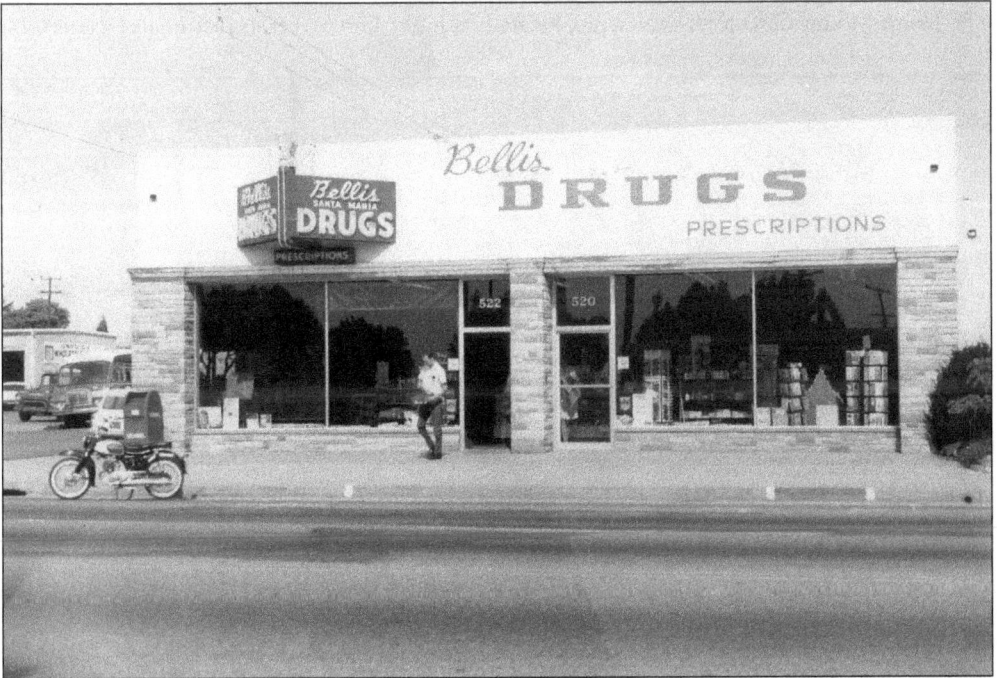

Bellis Drugs on North Broadway was a popular neighborhood drugstore that also sold costume jewelry and unique novelties.

The Home Motors Chevrolet dealership, located on East Main Street, is pictured in the 1960s.

Bill Loper Ford, located on North Broadway, is shown in the mid-1950s.

At the corner of Church Street and Broadway in the mid-1970s are, from left to right, the B&B Café, Weaver's Camera Shop, Et Cetera, Christian Science Reading Room, Gardner's Rexall Drugs, Pant Works, the Corner, and a stereo shop. Across the street was the site of the January 30, 1945, crash of a P-38 aircraft during a military exercise. It directly hit the Rusconi Café and damaged the Economy Drug store next door.

The Guadalupe Railroad train station was built in 1892. Pam Bondietti is pictured at the station in 1972. (Courtesy of Rancho de Guadalupe Historical Society & Museum.)

This is the intersection of Broadway and Main Street, where the town's first flagpole was erected in 1918, in the early 1950s. Floral-covered islands ran down the middle of the street, separating north- and southbound traffic.

Tom-Don Roller-Drome was the town's roller rink in the 1950s and 1960s. (Courtesy of the author.)

Shown here in the 1940s, the Massy Hotel, located on West Main Street, later became the Palms Motor Motel. (Courtesy of the author.)

Several stores can be seen in this 1950s Elks Parade on Broadway. From front to back are Prindles Western Wear, Economy Drug, Coffee Cup, Santa Maria News Stand, Bradley Hotel, Rex Café, several various small cafés, Western Union, and Johnson Chevrolet and garage. (Courtesy of Santa Maria Elks Lodge 1538 History Committee.)

House of Fabrics in Santa Maria is pictured in the 1960s.

The Vandenberg Hotel on Broadway and Stowell Road is seen in the 1960s. It was a full-service hotel with a coffee shop, restaurant, and cocktail lounge. The lodging later changed its name to the Vandenberg Inn, and its cocktail lounge became a popular nightclub that hosted live bands in the 1980s. (Courtesy of the author.)

Mussell Fort was established in 1952 by Elwin Mussell, a former Santa Maria mayor. The attraction was built on 574 acres, where Mussell re-created an old town with buildings that included Audrey's Alcove Room and Board House, a saloon, sheriff's office, and a general merchandise store. All of the buildings and props were original and were collected throughout the years by Mussell, who often traveled to several states in search of items.

The Santa Maria Post Office was once located on the southeast corner of Cypress and Lincoln Streets; it was demolished in the 1970s to make room for the West Side Mall.

The Santa Maria Speedway seen above was built in 1964 by Doug Fort and has been a popular racing arena since its opening. Below, a flagman on the track is directing racecars at a 1960s event. (Courtesy of Chris Kearns.)

Seven

A GLIMPSE AROUND TOWN
SANTA MARIA TODAY

It has been more than a century since the rancho era, but the adobe and Mission Revival–style architecture can still be seen in many of the city's newer and older buildings. Developments in the city have been ongoing in keeping up with an expanding population and a growing need for quality-of-life improvements. New offices, stores, and houses have slowly sprouted up on land where broccoli and lettuce were once grown. And unfortunate events through the years, such as the plane crash that destroyed the Rusconi Café in 1945 and the fire that destroyed the Bradley Hotel in 1970, have caused the destruction of some of the city's old buildings. In the 1970s, the construction of the Town Center Mall caused many old homes and businesses to be demolished, with some businesses relocating and others closing. But despite the new developments, the city memorializes its past, with many sites designated as historic landmarks and objects of historic merit. The City of Santa Maria has designated 11 sites as historic landmarks, including Buena Vista Park, located on Morrison and Pine Streets; the flagpole on the grounds at city hall, which was originally erected at the intersection of Main Street and Broadway; the Reuben Hart Home; the Pacific Coast Railroad depot site, on West Main Street and Railroad Avenue; Santa Maria Inn, located on South Broadway; Santa Maria City Hall, on East Cook Street; the Four Corners intersection of Main Street and Broadway; Veterans' Memorial Community Center, at Pine and Tunnell Streets; the site of the first Masonic Temple, on South Broadway; and the Santa Maria Cemetery District, on East Stowell Road. Objects of historic merit include Orange Street Kindergarten, "Old" St. Mary's Church, Cypress Street Kindergarten, Melby's Clock, the Coca-Cola Building, the historic bell at El Camino School, Leo's drive-in (now Taco Bell), the bas-relief of the ship *Santa Maria*, First United Methodist Church, St. Peter's Episcopal Church, Santa Maria Civic Theater, and the Zanetti/Twitchell home. There are many other places, too, that native Santa Marians and longtime residents will always remember and hold dear, places that can never be demolished or forgotten.

Santa Maria won an All-America City Award from the National Civic League in 1998. Established in 1949, this is one of the oldest recognition programs in the country, designed to acknowledge communities "whose citizens work in concert to identify and resolve community challenges and achieve uncommon results." The award is given annually to 10 cities in the United States. Seen here is the award displayed at city hall.

Mayor Laurence J. "Larry" Lavagnino is a native of Santa Maria and a graduate of both Santa Maria High School and Allan Hancock Community College. His long public-service career began in 1965, when he was a staff assistant to the county supervisors. He has served more than three terms on the Santa Maria City Council since 1996. (Courtesy of the City of Santa Maria.)

With funds from a $12,100 federal grant and $37,100 in municipal money saved by the city council, construction began on the Santa Maria City Hall in December 1933. Since its completion in 1934, city hall's Mission Revival–style architecture and manicured ground still grace the city.

A statue of a woman and boy was an artistic addition to the city hall courtyard.

The Ethel Pope Auditorium at Santa Maria High School is shown in 2011, long after the school's bell tower was removed in 1963.

Opened on August 23, 2008, the new Santa Maria Library is grand compared to back in 1907, when the Minerva Library Club was located in the lobby of one of the town's post offices and contained fewer than 600 books. The Minerva Club paved the path for a city library, beginning with the opening of a Carnegie library in 1909. In 1941, a new library was built next door to the old Carnegie library. It underwent three expansions, forcing the library during one expansion to temporarily relocate to an empty former Safeway supermarket for a year.

Located at the intersection of Broadway and Cook Street, near the heart of the city of Santa Maria, the First United Methodist Church was built in 1873. Although the church has undergone renovations throughout the years, its bell tower has remained and continues to be a city landmark.

Built in 1975, Union Plaza Apartments was the first high-rise building in the city. Bernett's Café was once located at the Union Plaza site.

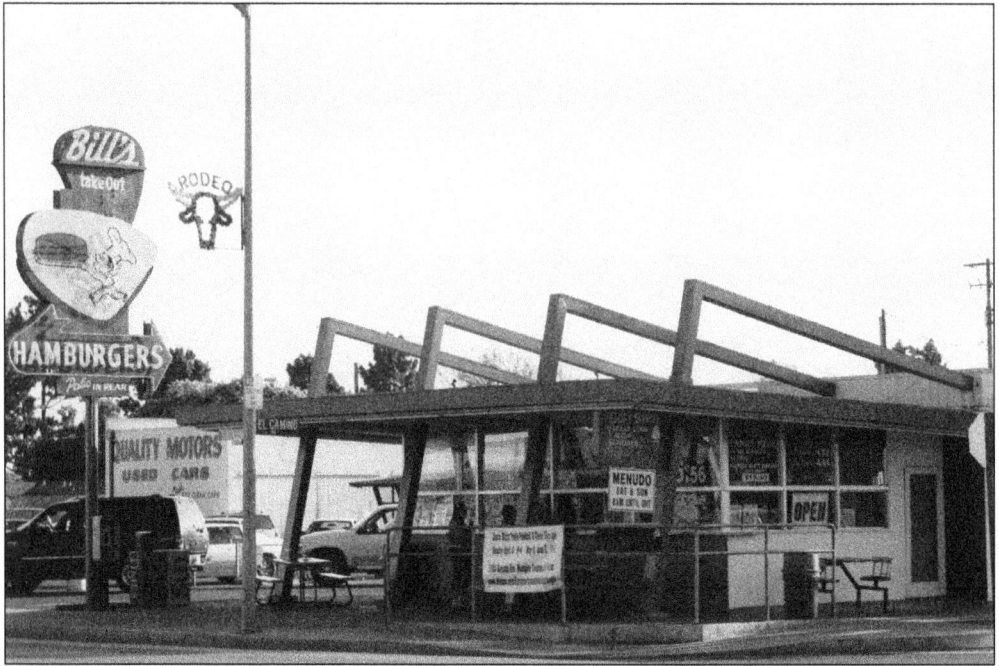

With the original sign still towering to the side the building, Bill's take-out hamburger stand, on North Broadway, has been a favorite among locals since the 1950s.

Established in the early 1960s, Casa Manana Mexican restaurant is still a local favorite on South Broadway. Neither its exterior nor interior has significantly changed in 50 years.

Pictured are the original (right) and newer water tanks in Guadalupe. After the 2003 San Simeon Earthquake, the smaller, 110-foot water tank that had served the community of Guadalupe since 1928 was deemed unsafe and was replaced with a new, larger tank. (Courtesy of Rancho de Guadalupe Historical Society & Museum.)

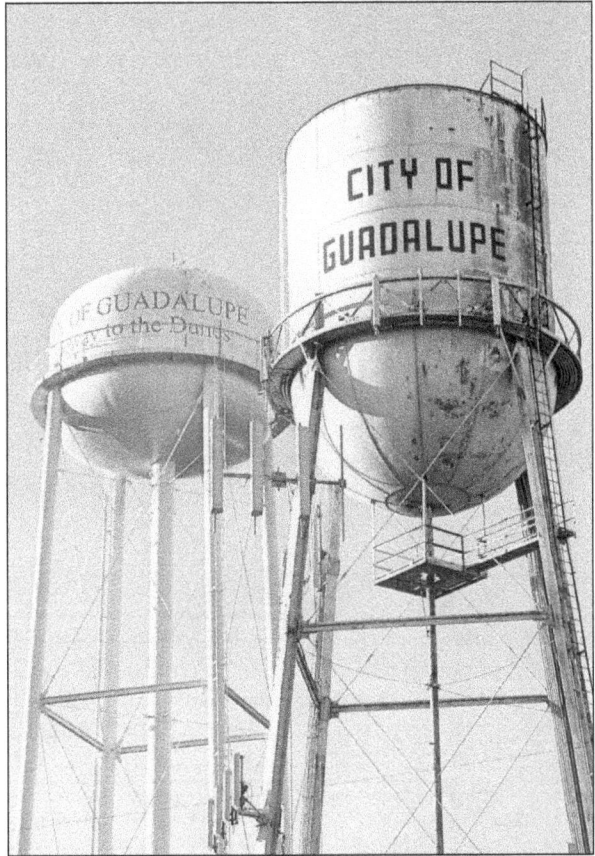

A field of broccoli lies along West Main Street in this view toward the hills north of Vandenberg. In the background, farm-equipment storage sheds are visible. Today, Guadalupe's landscape still consists of miles of agricultural farms.

Shown is the site of the Rancho de Guadalupe Historical Society, formed in 1989 by residents wishing to preserve the town's rich cultural and economic history, which spans more than a century. The group gained nonprofit status in 1993, and in 2002, a museum site was obtained in a room of the Veterans Memorial Building on Guadalupe Street and Highway 1.

This historic, landmark home in Guadalupe, built in 1902, was the second residence of the Campodonico family, one of the town's proprietary families in the late 1800s. The two-story Victorian structure has been well maintained throughout the years.

Guadalupe's Mission Revival–style city hall was built in the 1930s. It is the current location of Guadalupe's city hall, police station, and fire department.

Pictured is the old Guadalupe Jail, built in 1926. It was one of four original jails built in the county and is the only one that remains for historic preservation. It has two 2-bed cells and one holding cell.

Original buildings constructed in the 1920s still line Guadalupe Street in downtown Guadalupe. The building at right was built by the Richeda family in the early 1920s. The Richeda Building had stores downstairs and the family's living quarters upstairs.

The Far Western restaurant in Guadalupe was established in 1958 by the Minetti and Maretti families and has thrived for more than 50 years. The building was formerly the Palace Hotel, built in 1912 by Ercolina Forni and Bergam Carenini.

Now part of Guadalupe's civic center, this building, completed in 1930, was once the location of Guadalupe Joint Union School. Under a single roof, the school brought together students from four elementary schools. As part of the efforts of the Guadalupe Japanese Association, which recognized the need for funds, nine Japanese members raised $2,482 among themselves for the school within days.

This is the former site of the Campodonico Mercantile, one of the early businesses established in Guadalupe in the late 1800s. It is one of several original buildings still standing along downtown Guadalupe Street.

The Katayama clock still sits on the sidewalk in downtown Guadalupe, where the Katayama Jewelry store, built in 1923, was once located. Originally facing north and south, the clock was turned 90 degrees for travelers to see as they drive through town. After the bombing of Pearl Harbor, the clock was the target of vandalism. Constructed in 1939, the Royal Theater building in Guadalupe (below) was acquired by the city to be used for theatrical and community events. In earlier years, it was owned and operated by Moe Hernandez. In the 1950s, the theater showed Filipino- and Spanish-language films. To the left of the Royal Theater is the former site of Nakano Noodle restaurant, later the Snappy Lunch diner. To the left of Snappy Lunch is the site of the Hamasaki boardinghouse.

Opened in 1991, the Santa Barbara County Betteravia Government Center combined many formerly scattered county agencies into one complex.

County services that were once spread around the city were relocated to the center. The county treasurer-tax collector, health care services, probation offices, and county health clinic all occupy separate buildings within the complex.

The Landmark Square on South Broadway was formerly the Santa Maria Club, a men's club. Fred Pimentel, the Santa Maria Inn's longtime manager, became manager of the Santa Maria Club in 1950. It later became the Landmark Inn restaurant and bar.

Still in business at its original location on North Broadway and bearing its original sign dating back to the early 1960s, King Falafel has been a local favorite.

Old Town Orcutt is reminiscent of its founding days, back in 1904. The Orcutt Trade Center (above), located on the northwest block of Clark Avenue and Broadway, was originally the Orcutt Hotel, built around 1922. Local stories say that the hotel was built during Prohibition and was an outlet for selling whiskey. Next to the center is Anderson's. In addition to the existing Orcutt Trade Center, there are many other buildings around the town that date back to the early 1900s. Fire destroyed some original structures, and new buildings designed with Western-style facades took their place. Below, the Orcutt Trade Center includes the town's original Masonic building, a barbershop, Jack's in Old Orcutt, and Patricio's Pizzeria.

Old Town Market (above) was established in 2004 at the original site of Scolari's supermarket, which had opened in 1948. The market is reminiscent of an old country store; it not only sells groceries and wine but also has a large collection of antique furniture and collectibles at the back of the store (below).

Although the planting of grapes in California dates back to the Spanish era in the 1700s, when Franciscan monk Junipero Serra planted the first seeds at the early missions on the Central Coast, vineyards in the Santa Maria Valley began to appear when the wine industry came to the valley in the 1960s. Pictured is a vineyard with seemingly endless rows of grapevines extending over rolling hills. Today, miles of picturesque grapevines dot the landscape of the Santa Maria Valley.

Although the Santa Maria Valley is known for its agricultural industry, raising cattle has been a big part of its history that dates back to the Mexican ranchero era. Here, cattle are grazing along rolling hills.

The Guadalupe Vietnam War Memorial was dedicated on May 7, 2002, to honor local servicemen killed in action. A plaque on the flagpole bears the names of the honored soldiers. An El Camino Real mission bell can be seen to the right of the pole.

The Guadalupe Cemetery dates back to 1874, when the local Masons and Odd Fellows organizations purchased the property in which to bury their deceased members. It was deeded to the county in 1920. Over the years, it has become the town's cemetery.

On the right, longtime residents Richard and Sandra (née Nicolai) Chenoweth have deep roots in the valley. Richard's family arrived in the Santa Maria Valley in 1950. Sandra's family arrived in 1892. As director of the Santa Maria Valley Historical Society Museum, Richard has compiled and written several factual histories that are widely used at local community and museum tours, and he is acknowledged in many local history publications for his contributions to those works, including this book. Incorporated as a nonprofit organization in 1955, the Santa Maria Valley Historical Society was established to gather and preserve materials relating to the history of the Santa Maria Valley. Below is the society board of directors: from left to right, Gloria Mornard, Joanne McBride, Ginger Reeves, and Myrna Winter; (second row) Dee Martini, John Everett, Dave Cross, Jim Enos, Jim Zemaitis, Hal Madson, Dave Carey, and Shirley Contreras.

Visit us at
arcadiapublishing.com

www.ingramcontent.com/pod-product-compliance
Lightning Source LLC
Chambersburg PA
CBHW050551110426
42813CB00008B/2320